Fun with

MEXICAN
Cooking

PowerKiDS
press

New York

Published in 2010 by The Rosen Publishing Group, Inc.
29 East 21st Street, New York, NY 10010

U.S. Editor: Kara Murray

Photo Credits: All images by Marco Lanza and Walter Mericchi.

Library of Congress Cataloging-in-Publication Data

Ward, Karen, 1968–
  Fun with Mexican cooking / Karen Ward.
      p. cm. — (Let's get cooking!)
  Includes index.
  ISBN 978-1-4358-3452-1 (library binding) — ISBN 978-1-4358-3477-4 (pbk.) — ISBN 978-1-4358-3478-1 (6-pack)
  1. Cookery, Mexican—Juvenile literature. I. Title.
  TX945.5.H33W37 2010
  641.5972—dc22
                                        2009006793

Printed in the United States of America

CPSIA Compliance Information: Batch #BR018210PK: For Further Information contact Rosen Publishing, New York, New York at 1-800-237-9932

Contents

3

Introduction

Centuries ago, Mexico was home to native people such as the **Aztecs** and **Mayans**. These people made dishes using corn, chilies, and cocoa beans. When European settlers arrived in Mexico, they brought different styles of cooking. Today, Mexican food is a mixture of Spanish, French, Italian, and Native American recipes. Corn, chilies, tomatoes, beans, peppers, and avocados are all basic ingredients in Mexican cooking. The 14 recipes in this book are some of the most common Mexican dishes. Step-by-step photographs help explain each recipe. So enjoy, or as the Mexicans say, *"¡Buen provecho!"*

When cooking, you should always have an adult with you in the kitchen to help. Many of the tools used to prepare these recipes and others can be dangerous. Always be very careful when using a knife or a stove.

Tortillas and Eggs

This dish is called *chilaquiles* (chee-lah-KEE-les). In Mexico, it is often served for breakfast. Tortillas can be made from corn or wheat. Here we use corn tortillas. This recipe includes vegetables, but chilaquiles can also be made without them. Eating chilaquiles is a great way to start the day!

4

1 Place one tortilla on the cutting board. Using a knife, cut it into bite-size pieces. Do this for all six tortillas. Now peel the skin off of the onion. Chop the onion, tomato, and bell pepper into small pieces.

2 Break all the eggs into a bowl. Add the salt and pepper to the eggs. Use a fork or whisk to beat the eggs until they are **frothy**. Set them aside for later use.

Utensils

KNIFE

CUTTING BOARD

LARGE SPOON

LARGE SKILLET OR FRYING PAN

3 Place a large frying pan on the stove. Turn the heat up to medium. Add half the vegetable oil. Wait one minute and add the onion and tortillas. Cook and stir until the onion and tortillas brown slightly. Add the remaining oil. Raise the heat to medium hot. Wait about 1 minute, until the oil is hot, then add the peppers. Wait another minute and add the tomatoes.

4 Stir and cook until the vegetables are soft and the tortillas are a light golden brown and crispy. Add the egg mixture and continue stirring until the eggs are cooked. Serve right away!

TIPS & TRICKS

Hot oil can splatter and burn you. Be careful when adding food to the frying pan. Hold the plate with the food just above the pan. Use the wooden spoon to slip the food into the pan so that none of the oil splatters onto your hands. When stirring the food, hold the pan handle firmly with your other hand.

Ingredients

6 small corn tortillas

1 small onion

1 small tomato

1 bell pepper

6 eggs

1 teaspoon salt

1 teaspoon pepper

2 tablespoons vegetable oil

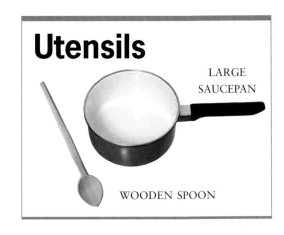

Hot Chocolate

Chocolate originally came from Mexico. It is made from the beans of the cocoa tree, which the Aztecs used in their cooking. When Spanish explorer Hernán Cortés met the Aztec ruler Montezuma in 1519, he was served a bitter cocoa drink called *xocoatl*. Cortés then introduced this drink to Spain.

Utensils

LARGE SAUCEPAN

WOODEN SPOON

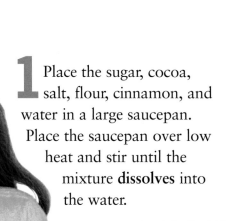

1 Place the sugar, cocoa, salt, flour, cinnamon, and water in a large saucepan. Place the saucepan over low heat and stir until the mixture **dissolves** into the water.

For a quick and easy version of this recipe, follow these instructions. In a pot, boil 4 cups (1 l) of milk. Add one tablet of Abuelita brand Mexican chocolate. Stir until the tablet dissolves in the milk. Sprinkle with cinnamon and serve hot.

2 After the mixture is dissolved, turn the stove up to medium high. Stir the mixture until it boils. Boil for 3 to 5 minutes, stirring all the time.

3 Add the milk. Continue to stir until the milk is hot but not boiling.

4 Just before the milk boils, remove the saucepan from the heat. Stir in the vanilla extract, and serve!

Ingredients

½ cup (120 ml) sugar

¼ cup (60 ml) cocoa

¼ **teaspoon** salt

1 tablespoon all-purpose flour

1 teaspoon cinnamon

1 cup (240 ml) cold water

4 cups (1 l) milk

2 teaspoons vanilla extract

Tortilla Soup

This is a classic Mexican soup. There are two types of soups in Mexico. Dry soups are full of rice or noodles that soak up the broth while they are cooking. Wet soups are like the soups that Americans and Canadians usually eat. Tortilla soup is a wet soup made with chicken stock. You can make the chicken stock beforehand by adding a chicken bouillon cube to boiling water and stirring until it dissolves.

1 Chop the onion, garlic, celery, and zucchini into small pieces.

2 Warm a saucepan over medium heat. Once the saucepan is hot, add the oil and vegetables to it. Cook until the vegetables are soft.

TIPS & TRICKS

It is usually best to do all the cutting and chopping before you begin cooking. Then you will have everything ready when you need it. When chopping ingredients, try to cut them all about the same size. This technique allows all the pieces to be cooked evenly.

Utensils

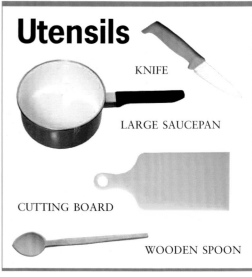

KNIFE

LARGE SAUCEPAN

CUTTING BOARD

WOODEN SPOON

Ingredients

 ½ onion

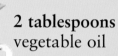 2 cloves garlic

1 stalk celery

 2 small zucchini

2 tablespoons vegetable oil

2 cups (500 ml) crushed tomatoes

 1 cup (250 ml) water

 2 cups (500 ml) chicken stock

1 cup (250 ml) cooked corn

½ teaspoon cumin

 corn tortilla strips or chips

 1 avocado

3 Add all the other ingredients, except the avocado and tortilla strips. Stir often and **simmer** over low heat for 30 minutes.

4 When you are ready to serve, slice the avocado. Ladle the soup into individual bowls. Add some avocado and chips to each one, and serve.

Beef and Potato Soup

This soup is called *caldito* (kahl-DEE-toh). It is a soup that Mexicans say tastes even better the next day! This is a great dish to make if you are planning to invite friends for a meal and have a number of recipes to prepare. Make the caldito the day before and just reheat it before serving. Caldito is a perfect soup for winter evenings. As an extra touch, try adding some sliced green onions right before serving.

Utensils

KNIFE

LARGE SKILLET OR FRYING PAN

CUTTING BOARD

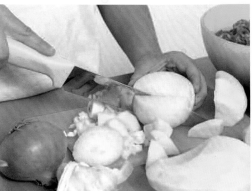

1 Chop the onion and fresh chilies (if you are using them instead of canned chilies). **Mince** the garlic, and **dice** the potatoes.

2 Place the beef, onion, potatoes, and garlic in a large frying pan over medium heat. Stir and cook until the meat is browned. Make sure there is no pink left in the meat. Drain any liquid that has formed in the pan. Ask an adult to help you. Remember the pan will be heavy and hot!

4 Add the water or chicken stock and stir well.

5 Add the green chilies and stir. Simmer over low heat for 30 minutes.

3 Return the meat mixture to the pan. The stove should remain at medium heat. Stir until the potatoes start to soften.

Ingredients

½ medium onion

2 cloves garlic

5 medium potatoes

1 pound (450 g) ground beef

2 small cans chopped green chilies or **8 to 10 fresh** chilies, roasted, peeled, **veined,** and seeded

3 cups (700 ml) water or chicken stock

TIPS & TRICKS

When in the kitchen, make sure you are not wearing long, loose clothing that may get caught on a handle or near a flame. Wear an apron to protect your clothes. Before opening cans of food, rinse the tops to remove any dust sitting on top.

6 The next day, reheat and serve hot with tortillas.

Guacamole

(gwah-kah-MOH-leh)

Guacamole is a dip made of mashed avocados. It is flavored with chilies and lime or lemon juice and often has chopped tomatoes, green onion, and **cilantro**. The word "guacamole" comes from two Aztec words, *aguacate* meaning "avocado" and *mole* meaning "mixture." Some Mexican cities have their own ways of serving guacamole. In Monterrey, the tomatoes and onions are served as a **garnish** so that the dish looks like the red, white, and green stripes on the Mexican flag.

1 Cut the avocados in half lengthwise. Remove the pits.

2 Use a spoon to hollow out the green, fleshy part of the avocados. Put the flesh into the bowl.

TIPS & TRICKS

Many recipes in this book have you use a sharp knife for chopping and cutting ingredients. Take care when choosing the right knife. Talk to an adult about which is the best and safest knife in your kitchen for each job. When using a knife, hold it firmly in one hand and hold the ingredient in the other. Be sure that your fingers are not in the way of the blade.

3 Mash the avocado flesh using the back part of a fork. Add the lemon juice and salt. Stir.

4 Chop the green onion and the green chili. Peel and mince the garlic. Add the onion, garlic, and chilies to the avocado and stir well.

Utensils

BOWL

CUTTING BOARD

KNIFE

5 Chop the tomato into small pieces. Add the pieces to the avocado and stir well.

6 Place the guacamole in a serving dish. Serve with corn chips as a dip.

Ingredients

2 avocados

½ **teaspoon** salt

2 **teaspoons** lemon or lime juice

½ tomato

2 cloves garlic

1 green onion

2 **tablespoons** green chili

Salsa

(SAHL-sah)

¡Caliente! means "hot!" That is the best way to describe this famous sauce. Salsa is a mixture of tomatoes, onions, chilies, and other ingredients. Salsa is served all over Mexico with tortillas and grilled meats, fish, or rice. It is also a popular appetizer served with a bowl of tortilla chips. This dish is best made during the hot summer months, when tomatoes are ripe.

The inside veins and seeds of a jalapeño are very hot. If you have them, use rubber gloves when chopping jalapeño peppers. Make sure you do not rub your eyes, and wash your hands with soap after handling the peppers.

1 Chop the onion, cilantro, and tomatoes. Place them in a small bowl.

2 Finely chop the jalapeño and add it to the bowl. Keep your hands away from your eyes.

Utensils

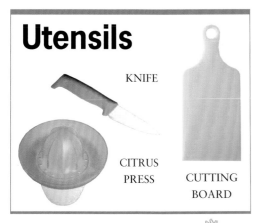

KNIFE

CITRUS
PRESS

CUTTING
BOARD

TIPS & TRICKS

*Always wash your hands before you start to cook. When using fruits and vegetables, always rinse them under cold running water before cutting them. Washing the food helps remove harmful **pesticides**. Even fruit of which you only use the insides, such as lemons or limes, should be rinsed before using them.*

3 Squeeze the limes, then pour the juice into the bowl with the tomatoes. Be careful to remove the lime seeds, which are very bitter. Add the salt and mix well.

4 Place the salsa in a serving dish. Serve with chips or as a sauce. The salsa will taste best if made the day before

Ingredients

1 onion

½ bunch cilantro

2 tomatoes

1 large
jalapeño pepper

3 limes

½ teaspoon
salt

The Day of the Dead

One of the most important festivals in Mexico is the *Día de los muertos*, which means the Day of the Dead. This festival is held on November 2. The Day of the Dead combines ancient Aztec traditions with celebrations of the Spanish Roman Catholics who settled in Mexico during the 1500s. The original Aztec celebrations were held during August. These festivities were dedicated to children and the dead. Spanish priests moved these celebrations to November so that they happened during Roman Catholic feast days. Today, Mexicans celebrate *Día de los muertos* by meeting together in the cemeteries where their relatives are buried.

Bread of the Dead

- ¼ cup (60 ml) milk
- ¼ cup (60 ml) butter
- ¼ cup (60 ml) warm water
- 3 cups (700 ml) all-purpose flour
- 1 ¼ teaspoons active dry yeast
- ½ teaspoon salt
- 2 teaspoons anise seed
- ½ cup (120 ml) sugar
- 2 eggs, beaten
- 2 teaspoons orange zest
- ¼ cup fresh orange juice
- 1 tablespoon orange zest

*Heat milk and butter in a saucepan until butter melts. Remove from heat and add the water. Combine 1 cup (250 ml) of flour, yeast, salt, anise seed, and half the sugar in a large bowl. Stir in the milk mixture. Add the eggs and beat until well mixed. Stir in ¹/₂ cup (120 ml) of flour and continue adding flour until the dough is soft. Place on a floured surface and **knead** until smooth and elastic. Place the dough in a bowl and cover with a cloth. Let rise in a warm place until it has doubled in size (about 1 hour). Shape the dough into a large round loaf with a round knob on top. Place on a baking sheet, cover with a cloth, and let rise in a warm place for 1 hour. Bake in a preheated 350°F (180°C) oven for about 40 minutes. To make glaze: In a small saucepan, combine remaining sugar with orange juice and zest. Bring to a boil over medium heat and boil for 2 minutes. Brush over bread while still warm.*

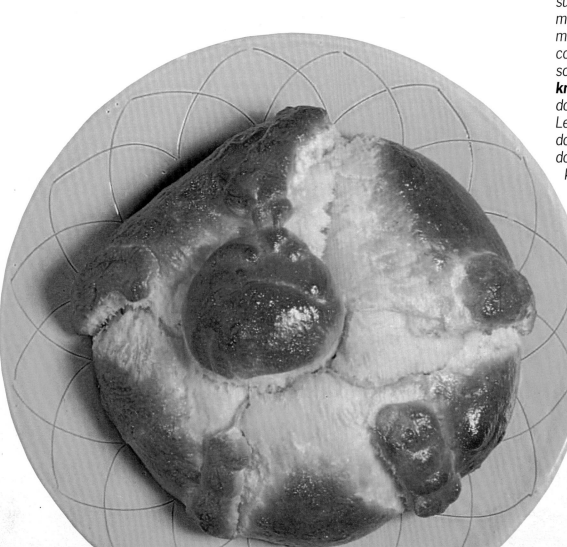

Many people hide a tiny plastic skeleton or skull inside each *pan de muerto*, or bread of the dead. It is good luck if you are the one to find it.

For the ancient Aztecs, death was not a sad event. It was just another stage of the human journey. Today, when Mexicans gather in their homes or cemeteries to celebrate the Day of the Dead, they eat well and enjoy one another's company. They also spend time remembering their dead relatives.

During the Day of the Dead, friends and family give one another gifts such as sugar skulls (like the ones above) or other things related to death. People write the receiver's name on gifts.

The Day of the Dead is celebrated in different ways in the many regions of Mexico. In the southwestern region of Oaxaca, for example, the dead are actually worshipped during the ceremonies. But in most large cities, this holiday is a family day when people get together and share special foods.

Wheat-Flour Tortillas

Tortilla means "small and flattened" in Spanish. Tortillas can be made from wheat or corn flour. Wheat-flour tortillas are more common in the northern states of Mexico. When serving tortillas, remember that they are the best when they are hot.

Utensils

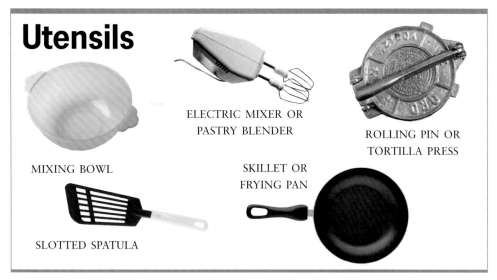

MIXING BOWL

ELECTRIC MIXER OR
PASTRY BLENDER

ROLLING PIN OR
TORTILLA PRESS

SLOTTED SPATULA

SKILLET OR
FRYING PAN

1 Place the flour, salt, and baking powder into a mixing bowl. Add the shortening to this mixture. Use an electric mixer to blend this mixture together. This process is called cutting the shortening. The dough will be coarse when it is ready.

2 Add the hot water to the dough a little at a time. Use your hands to blend it together until the dough is smooth. Put some flour on a clean surface and place the dough on it. Put flour on your hands and knead the dough about 20 times. Leave it for 10 minutes.

3 Take a piece of dough about the size of an egg and shape it into a ball.

4 Use a rolling pin or a tortilla press to flatten the ball into a tortilla about 6 inches (15 cm) wide. Repeat steps 3 and 4 until all the dough has been used.

5 Heat a frying pan to medium heat. Cook a tortilla for about 2 minutes until it starts to turn light brown.

6 Use a spatula to flip the tortilla. Cook for 2 more minutes. Remove the tortilla. Repeat until all the tortillas are cooked.

TIPS & TRICKS

To keep the tortillas warm, put a clean dish towel on a plate. Place the warm tortilla on the dish towel and cover it with the other end of the towel. You can also warm tortillas in the oven at 200°F (100°C).

Ingredients

4 cups (1 l) all-purpose flour

2 teaspoons salt

2 teaspoons baking powder

4 tablespoons shortening

1½ cups (350 ml) hot water

Mexican Rice

Rice was introduced to Mexico by the Spanish. It has become very popular and is used in appetizers, main courses, and desserts. This rice and vegetable dish is filling enough to be served on its own for dinner. If you like spicy food, try serving this with the salsa recipe on page 14.

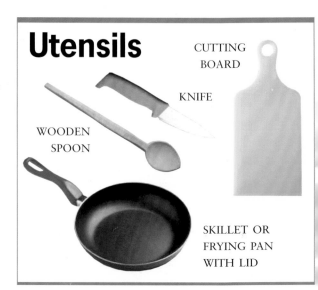

1 Chop the onion, tomatoes, and bell pepper. Measure 2 cups (500 ml) water. Set aside the vegetables and water until later.

2 Place a frying pan on the stove at medium heat. Add the oil to the pan and warm it up. Add the rice and stir until it is light brown.

Utensils

CUTTING BOARD

KNIFE

WOODEN SPOON

SKILLET OR FRYING PAN WITH LID

3 Add vegetables and stir until they are tender but not mushy.

4 Add the bouillon cube and water. Stir. When the water begins to simmer, cover the pan with the lid. Cook 12 to 15 minutes or until the rice begins to curl and becomes soft. Serve hot.

TIPS & TRICKS

Use a long-handled wooden spoon to stir the rice. It will keep the heat away from your hand, and it will not damage the surface of your frying pan. While stirring, make sure that you scrape every part of the bottom of the pan. Occasionally, scrape the sides of the pan to make sure everything is mixed together.

Ingredients

1 onion

2 tomatoes

1 green bell pepper

1 tablespoon vegetable oil

2 cups (500 ml) rice

2 cups (500 ml) water

1 vegetable or chicken bouillon cube

Pinto Beans with Tomato and Bacon

Beans are **native** to Mexico and are one of the country's most common foods. There are many recipes with beans as the main ingredient. In Mexico, beans are often cooked in large clay pots. These pots give the beans a special flavor. We suggest you use a pressure cooker or a pot with a tight lid. In this recipe, we use dried pinto beans. These beans require soaking overnight before they are used.

1 Carefully sort through the dried beans. Throw away any beans that are wrinkled or cracked. Pick out any small stones.

2 Place the beans in a bowl and cover them with water. Soak them overnight. Then, drain the water and place the beans in the pressure cooker.

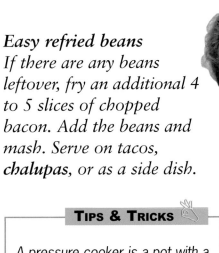

4 Cook for about 1 hour, or until the beans are plump and soft. Check the pot often to make sure there is water covering the beans. Ask an adult to help you when lifting the lid.

Utensils

CUTTING BOARD

KNIFE

PRESSURE COOKER OR POT WITH LID

23

3 Chop the garlic and bacon. Add them to the pressure cooker. Add the tomatoes, salt, and enough water to just cover the beans. Cover with the lid and bring to a boil.

Easy refried beans
If there are any beans leftover, fry an additional 4 to 5 slices of chopped bacon. Add the beans and mash. Serve on tacos, **chalupas,** *or as a side dish.*

Ingredients

3 cups (700 g) dried pinto beans

1 clove garlic

3 slices bacon

2 cups (500 ml) crushed tomatoes

½ teaspoon salt

cold water, as required

TIPS & TRICKS

A pressure cooker is a pot with a locking lid and a valve from which steam can escape. Food cooks quickly in these pots. If you do not have one in your kitchen, just use a large, deep saucepan with a tight-fitting lid. Beans cooked in this type of pot will take about 2 hours to cook.

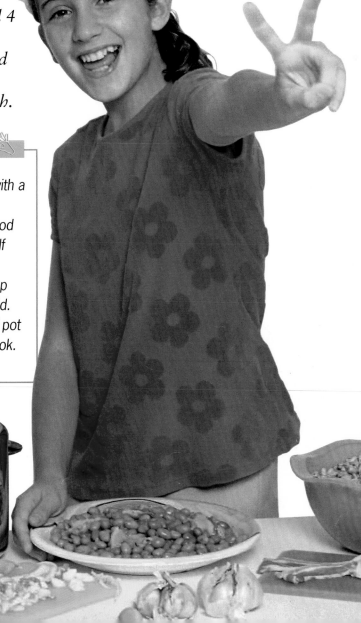

Tacos

Tacos make a tasty lunch or snack. You can prepare the fillings ahead of time. Make sure you fill the taco shells just before serving so that they stay crunchy. Add salsa (pages 14–15) to your tacos for extra flavor. Taco filling also tastes great on top of a tostada. To make a tostada, fry a tortilla flat instead of in a curved pocket.

24

Utensils

WOODEN SPOON

CHEESE GRATER

CUTTING BOARD

KNIFE

SKILLET OR
FRYING PAN

Ingredients

1 small onion

2 ripe tomatoes

1 head of lettuce, washed

1–2 cloves garlic

1 pound (450 g) ground beef

1 teaspoon salt

1½ teaspoons chili powder (optional)

10 to 12 hard taco shells

1 cup (250 ml) cooked beans drained or refried beans

1½ cups (350 ml) grated cheddar cheese

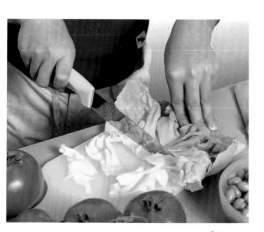

1 Chop the onion, tomatoes, lettuce, and garlic and set them aside.

2 Place a frying pan over the stove on medium heat. Add the beef, garlic, salt, and chili powder to the pan. If you are using cooked beans, add these to the pan as well. Cook and stir until the meat is brown. Make sure there is no pink left in the meat. Drain away any liquid from the

meat.

3 Fill the taco shells with meat, beans, lettuce, tomato, and onion.

4 Top with grated cheddar cheese. Cover with spoonfuls of spicy salsa, if you like.

TIPS & TRICKS

If you cannot find crunchy taco shells, ask an adult to make them for you. Heat 1 inch (2.5 cm) of oil in a frying pan on medium high heat. Place a corn tortilla in the hot oil. Use tongs to fold it over. Fry one side and then the other. Drain the shells on paper towels.

Churritos

(choo-REE-tohs)

These sweet tortilla fritters can be served on their own as a tasty treat. They are also great with vanilla ice cream. If you want to make a healthier dessert, you can bake churritos in the oven. Preheat the oven to 350°F (180°C). Cut the tortillas into ½-inch (1 cm) strips. Twist the strips and place them on a lightly greased cookie sheet. Sprinkle with cinnamon and sugar and bake in the oven until they are crunchy.

Utensils

SKILLET OR FRYING PAN

SLOTTED SPATULA

KNIFE

CUTTING BOARD

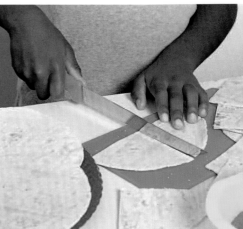

1 Cut the tortillas into quarters. Heat the oil in a frying pan over medium high heat.

2 Carefully place the tortillas in the pan. Be careful! The oil is very hot. It could splatter on your hands and arms and cause painful burns. Ask an adult to help and watch you.

3 Fry the tortillas until they are golden on both sides. Place the cooked tortillas on paper towels. Repeat until all the tortillas are fried.

4 Sprinkle the tortillas with cinnamon and sugar. Serve while still hot!

Ingredients

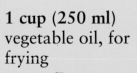

4 small wheat-flour tortillas

1 cup (250 ml) vegetable oil, for frying

cinnamon to taste

½ cup (125 ml) sugar

TIPS & TRICKS

When cooking, make sure that the handles of pots and pans do not hang over the edge of the stove. Turn the handles in so that they will not get bumped. Never leave the kitchen when you have oil on the stove. It can catch fire. If it does, turn off the heat and leave the kitchen at once. Find an adult to help you put out the flames.

Flan

(FLAHN)

This baked custard dessert is cooked in the oven using a technique called **bain-marie**. To cook using bain-marie, the pan with the food is placed inside a larger, deeper pan that is filled with water. As the water is heated, it creates steam in the oven that is just right for baking custards.

Utensils

ELECTRIC MIXER

MIXING BOWL

LARGE PAN (SHOULD BE MUCH LARGER THAN THE BAKING DISH)

1-QUART (1 L) BAKING DISH

1 Preheat the oven to 350°F (180°C). Spread a thin layer of butter inside the baking dish. Break four eggs and place them in a mixing bowl. Beat the eggs with an electric mixer until they are smooth.

2 Add the milk, cream, sugar, and vanilla to the eggs.

TIPS & TRICKS

When putting things into or taking them out of the oven, always wear thick, protective oven mitts. If the dish in the oven is heavy, ask an adult to help you move it. When you are finished cooking, be sure to clean up the kitchen. Cleaning helps keep germs out of your kitchen and your food.

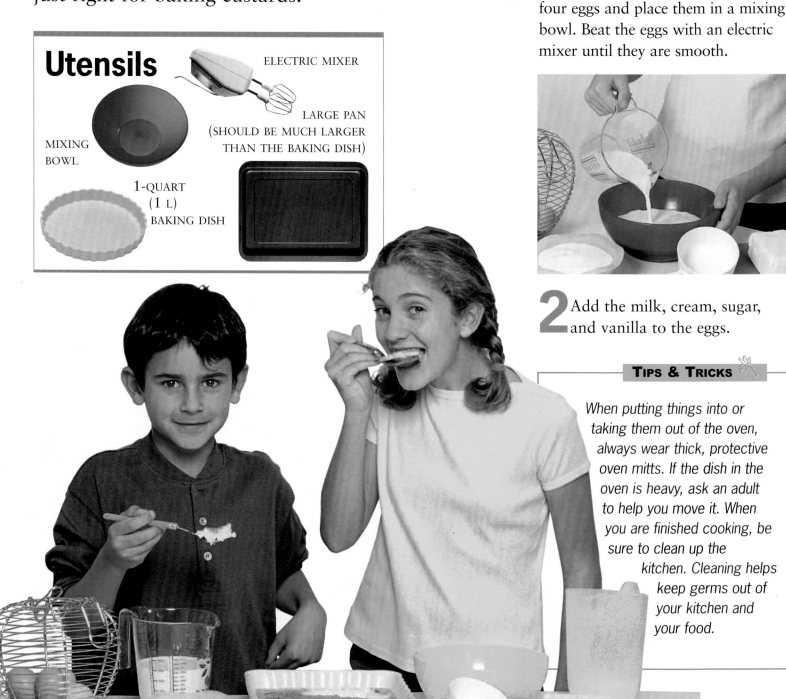

3 Beat with the electric mixer until well mixed. The mixture should be smooth and creamy.

4 Gently pour this mixture into the baking dish. Scrape the sides of the bowl to get out all of the mixture. Place the baking dish into the larger pan. Use a cup and fill the larger pan with hot water so that it comes up around the edge of the smaller dish.

Ingredients

butter, to grease the baking dish

4 eggs

1 cup (250 ml) milk

1 cup (250 ml) light cream

½ cup (125 ml) granulated sugar

1 teaspoon vanilla extract

½ cup (125 ml) brown sugar

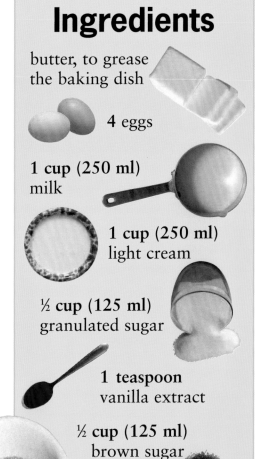

5 Place the pans into the oven. Ask an adult to help you because the water may spill out. Bake for 1 hour. Place a toothpick into the center of the flan. If the toothpick comes out clean, the flan is cooked. Remove the flan, let it cool, then chill it in the refrigerator for several hours.

6 Make sure the oven rack is about 8 inches (20 cm) from the top of the oven. Turn the oven on to broil. Sprinkle the top of the flan with brown sugar. Ask an adult to help you place it into the oven. Broil until it is light brown and the sugar starts to melt. Have someone help you remove it from the oven. Serve immediately.

Rice Pudding

Rice pudding is a dessert commonly served in Mexico. The pudding can be served chilled or while it is still warm, with ice cream. Another way to serve it is to cook the pudding until it is very thick. Roll the pudding into balls and fry them until golden brown. Sprinkle the balls with cinnamon and sugar and serve warm.

1 Combine the rice, **evaporated milk**, sugar, and egg yolks in a saucepan over medium heat. Stir.

2 Add the vanilla extract, raisins, and spices. Simmer for 5 minutes over low heat. Remove from the heat.

3 Beat the egg whites with a mixer until they are stiff. Scoop the egg whites carefully into the rice mixture.

Utensils

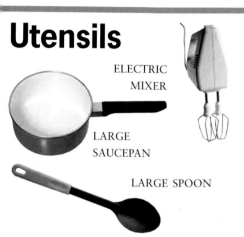

ELECTRIC MIXER

LARGE SAUCEPAN

LARGE SPOON

4 Spoon the mixture into bowls. Sprinkle with the cinnamon and place in the refrigerator for at least 2 hours. Serve when chilled.

Ingredients

 1 cup (250 ml) cooked rice

 2 cups (500 ml) evaporated milk

GLORIA
EVAPORADA

 ¾ cup (175 ml) granulated sugar

 1 cup (250 ml) raisins

 3 eggs, separated

1 teaspoon vanilla extract

 ¼ teaspoon cinnamon

¼ teaspoon nutmeg

TIPS & TRICKS

If you do not have an egg separator, you can do it yourself. Crack the egg over the bowl. Gently pour the egg into half of the shell without breaking the yolk (the yellow part). Allow the white to slide into the bowl. Repeat until all the yolk and whites are separated. Put the yolks in a separate bowl from the whites.

Glossary

Aztecs (AZ-teks) An ethnic group that ruled much of Mexico before the Spanish arrived in 1521.

bain-marie (ban-muh-REE) A technique that uses a water bath to gently cook or steam food.

chalupas (chah-LOO-pahs) Fried, curved tortillas.

cilantro (sih-LAHN-troh) An herb used in cooking.

dice (DYS) To cut food into tiny cubes using a knife.

dissolved (dih-ZOLVD) When something, such as salt, is mixed into a liquid, such as water.

evaporated milk (ih-VA-puh-rayt-ed MILK) Unsweetened, canned milk that has had its water removed by evaporation.

frothy (FRAW-thee) Describing a liquid that has been shaken or stirred until bubbles form.

garnish (GAHR-nish) A portion of food added to the side of a dish as decoration.

knead (NEED) To mix and smooth out dough before it is baked.

Mayans (MY-unz) An ethnic group that was one of the first peoples to live in Mexico.

mince (MINTS) To cut or chop into very small pieces.

native (NAY-tiv) From a certain area or country.

pesticides (PES-tuh-sydz) Chemicals farmers use to kill insects and pests that eat crops.

separated (SEH-puh-rayt-ed) Divided an egg's yolk from its white, both to be used at different stages of a recipe.

simmer (SIH-mer) To cook just at or below a liquid's boiling point.

veined (VAYN-ed) Removed the veins from a vegetable such as a chili pepper.

Index

Web Sites

Due to the changing nature of Internet links, PowerKids Press has developed an online list of Web sites related to the subject of this book. This site is updated regularly. Please use this link to access the list: www.powerkidslinks.com/lgc/mexican/